D0638455

A dog is the only thing on earth
that will love you more than you love yourself
Josh Billings (1818-1885)

First published in 2005 by
Bizzybee Publishing Ltd
Briarbank · Mansfield Road · Farnsfield
Nottinghamshire NG22 8HH
www.bizzybeepublishing.biz
© bizzybee publishing limited 2005

Reprinted in 2006 & 2007
Printed and bound in China

A watchdog is a dog kept to guard your home, usually by sleeping where a burglar would awaken the household by falling over him.

Author Unknown

Money will buy a
pretty good dog
but it won't buy
the wag of his tail.

Josh Billings
(1818-1885)

When you tire of puppies...

you tire of life!

The more I see
of the depressing stature of people,
the more I admire my dogs.
Alphonse de Lamartine (1790-1869)

His name is not wild dog anymore, but the first friend, because he will be our friend for always and always and always.
Rudyard Kipling (1865-1936)

A good dog deserves a good bone.

American Proverb

If a dog's prayers were
answered, bones would
rain from the sky.

Old Proverb

Every boy should have
two things: a dog,
and a mother willing
to let him have one.

Author Unknown

The dog was created especially
for children.
He is the god of frolic.
Henry Ward Beecher (1813-1887)

It's no coincidence that man's best friend cannot talk.

Author Unknown

He is your friend, your partner, your defender, your dog. You are his life, his love, his leader.

Author Unknown

One reason a dog is such a
lovable creature is
his tail wags instead
of his tongue.

Author Unknown

When man is in trouble, God sends him a dog.

Alphonse de Lamartine
(1790-1869)

Here, Gentlemen, a dog teaches us
a lesson in humanity.

Napoleon Bonaparte
(1769-1821)

Brothers and sisters, I bid you beware
Of giving your heart to a dog to tear.

Rudyard Kipling
(1865-1936)

He will be yours, faithful and true, to the last beat of his heart. You owe it to him to be worthy of such devotion.

Author Unknown

The best part about owning a dog is the way he doesn't care about bad hair days or overdue bills.

Author Unknown

A dog owns nothing,
yet is seldom dissatisfied.
Irish Proverb

You think dogs will not be in heaven? I tell you, they will be there long before any of us.

Robert Louis Stevenson (1850-1894)

My dog, she looks at me
sometimes with that look,
and I think maybe deep down
inside she must know
exactly how I feel.
But then maybe she just wants
the food off my plate.

Author Unknown

...the Almighty... hath invested [the dog] with a nature noble and incapable of deceit.

Sir Walter Scott (1771-1832)

I'm sure God loves me, I know that is true.
He gave me so many great things to chew.

Author Unknown, from "The Life of a Puppy"

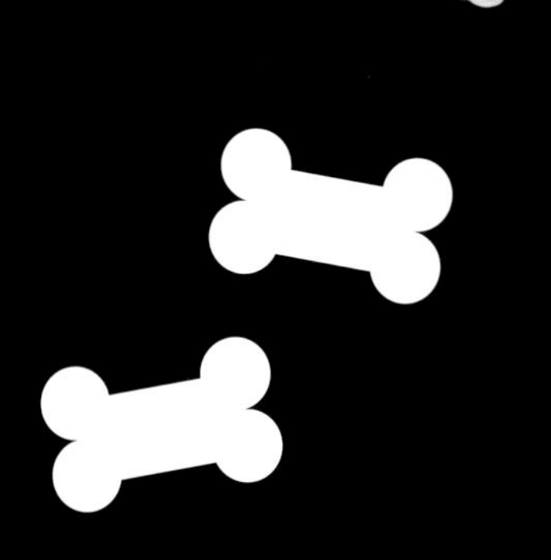

A dog is better than I am, for he has love and does not judge.
Saint Xanthias

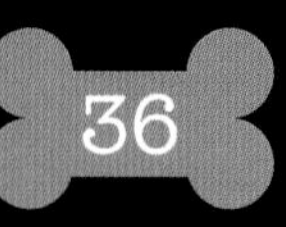

Dog, n. ...This Divine Being in some of his smaller and silkier incarnations takes, in the affection of Woman, the place to which there is no human male aspirant.

Ambrose Bierce (1842-1914), from "The Devil's Dictionary"

If your dog is fat, you aren't getting enough exercise.

Author Unknown

To err is human, to
forgive, canine.

Author Unknown

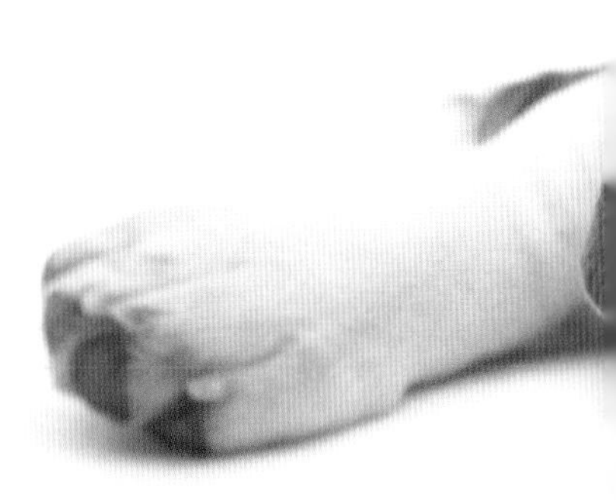

...dogs possess something very like a conscience.

Charles Darwin (1809-1882)

A puppy plays with every pup he meets....

Josh Billings (1818-1885)

All knowledge, the totality of
all questions and all answers
is contained in the dog.

Franz Kafka (1883-1924)

My hounds are bred out of the Spartan kind;
So flew'd, so sanded; their heads are hung
With ears that sweep away the morning dew...

William Shakespeare (1564-1616),
from "A Midsummer Night's Dream"

...you may make a fool of yourself with [a dog] and not only will he not scold you, but he will make a fool of himself, too.

Samuel Butler (1835-1902)

It's not the size of the dog in the fight,
it's the size of the fight in the dog.

Mark Twain (1835-1910)

[Dogs] never talk about themselves but listen to you while you talk about yourself, and keep up an appearance of being interested in the conversation.

Jerome K. Jerome (1859-1927)

Love me, love my dog.

George Chapman (c.1559-1634)

You must always remember that, as far as the Bible is concerned...

...God only threw the humans out of Paradise.

Author Unknown

He is gentle, he is kind –
I shall never, never find
A better friend than old dog Tray!
Stephen Collins Foster (1826-1864)

The greatest love is a mother's;
Then comes a dog's....
Polish Proverb

A dog has the soul of a philosopher.

Plato (c.428-c.348 BC)

If you pick up a starving dog and make him prosperous, he will not bite you. This is the principal difference between a dog and a man.

Mark Twain (1835-1910)

Buy a pup and your money will buy
Love unflinching that cannot lie...

Rudyard Kipling (1865-1936),
from "The Power of the Dog"

Every dog must have his day.
Jonathan Swift
(1667-1745)

The joy, the solace, and the aid of man....
George Crabbe (1754-1832)

The rich man's guardian
and the poor man's friend,
The only creature faithful to the end.

George Crabbe (1754-1832)

If a dog will not come to you after he has looked you in the face, you ought to go home and examine your conscience.

Woodrow Wilson (1856-1924)

My goal in life is to be as good a person as my dog already thinks I am.

Author Unknown

They are better than human
beings, because they know
but do not tell.

Emily Dickinson
(1830-1886)

Beauty without Vanity,
Strength without Insolence,
Courage without Ferocity,
and all the Virtues of Man without his Vices.

John Cam Hobhouse (1786-1869), epitaph to Lord Byron's dog, Boatswain

If my dog could talk
what a tale she could tell
she would probably tell me
my feet really smell!

Author Unknown

A dog can express more with his eyes in minutes than his owner can express with his tongue in hours.

Author Unknown

Never judge a dog's pedigree by the kind of books he does not chew.

Author Unknown

Like a lady's ringlets brown,
Flow thy silken ears adown
Either side demurely
Of thy silver-suited breast....

Elizabeth Barrett Browning (1806-1861),
from "To Flush, My Dog"

You always sympathize with the underdog, except when the other dog is yours.

Author Unknown

Make a special point every day
of teaching your dog
how to sit and stay
He will share your
laughter and your tears
and always be faithful
through the years....

Never be mean,
don't ever be cruel
He'll always be happy to
play the fool
Remember he loves you
with all of his might
So stroke and caress
him every night
Author Unknown

We hope that you have enjoyed this book, but please remember that owning a dog, or any pet, is a serious commitment. Animals need lots of love and attention, so please look after your pet responsibly.

The publisher would like to thank Warren Photographic for the use of their photographs.
All photographs © Warren Photographic